Just the Facts

Multiple
Sclerosis

Alexander Burnfield

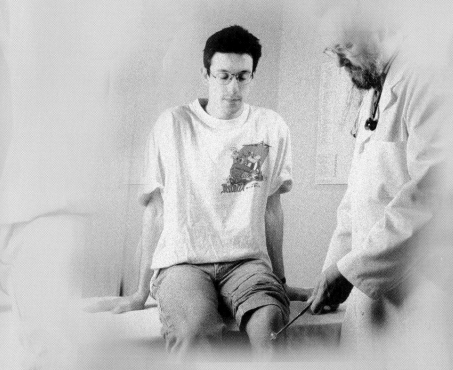

Heinemann Library
Chicago, Illinois

Customer Service 888-454-2279
Visit our website at www.heinemannlibrary.com

Produced by Monkey Puzzle Media
Designed by Jane Hawkins
Originated by Ambassador Litho Ltd.
Printed and bound in China by South China Printing Company

08 07 06 05 04
10 9 8 7 6 5 4 3 2 1

Library of Congress Cataloging-in-Publication Data
Burnfield, Alexander, 1944-
  Multiple sclerosis / Alexander Burnfield.
      p. cm. -- (Just the facts)
Summary: Describes the different types of MS, their symptoms, why this disease can be difficult to diagnose, various
types of treatment, and other issues related to multiple sclerosis.
Includes bibliographical references and index.
  ISBN 1-4034-4602-4 (lib. bdg. : hc)
  1. Multiple sclerosis--Juvenile literature. [1. Multiple sclerosis. 2.
Diseases.] I. Title. II. Series.
  RC377.B867 2003
  616.8'34--dc21
                              2003010913

Acknowledgments
The author and publisher are grateful to the following for permission to reproduce copyright material: pp. 1 (CC Studio),
4 (Custom Medical Stock Photo), 6 (Jon Meyer/Custom Medical Stock Photo), 7 (Athenais, ISM), 14 (CC Studio), 15 (Geoff
Tompkinson), 23 (Scott Camazine), 24, 25 (Dr. John Zajicek), 31 (BSIP Laurent), 32 (Claire Paxton and Jacqui Farrow), 34
(James King-Holmes), 39 (Peter Menzel), 47 (Philippe Plailly), 48 (James King-Holmes), 49 Science Photo Library; pp. 5
(Stone), 16 (Image Bank), 17 (Image Bank), 19 (Image Bank), 36–37 (Image Bank); Terence Keane p. 37 (National
Multiple Sclerosis Society) Getty Images; pp. 8–9 (Sigmund Freud Copyrights) Mary Evans Picture Library; pp. 10
(Hulton-Deutsch Collection), 20 (Paul Barton) Corbis; p. 13 (Crispin Hughes) Photofusion; pp. 27, 42 MS Trust; pp. 28, 29,
44–45, 50–51 Topham Picturepoint/ImageWorks; pp. 33 (Myrleen Cate/Photo Network), 41 (ImageState) Alamy; p. 43
(Helen Osler) Rex Features.

Cover photograph: main image (cells): Science Photo Library/Dr. John Zajicek; second image: Photofusion/Crispin Hughes

For more information on the images that appear on the cover of this book, turn to pages 13 and 25.

The author wishes to thank his wife, Penny, for her help in preparing the manuscript and his niece,
Catherine Reynell, for reading the manuscript. He is also grateful to the Multiple Sclerosis Trust and
Multiple Sclerosis International Federation for their help and to Ernest Hecht for his support. Special
thanks to Pamela G. Richards, M.Ed., for her help in the preparation of this book.

Contents

Multiple Sclerosis

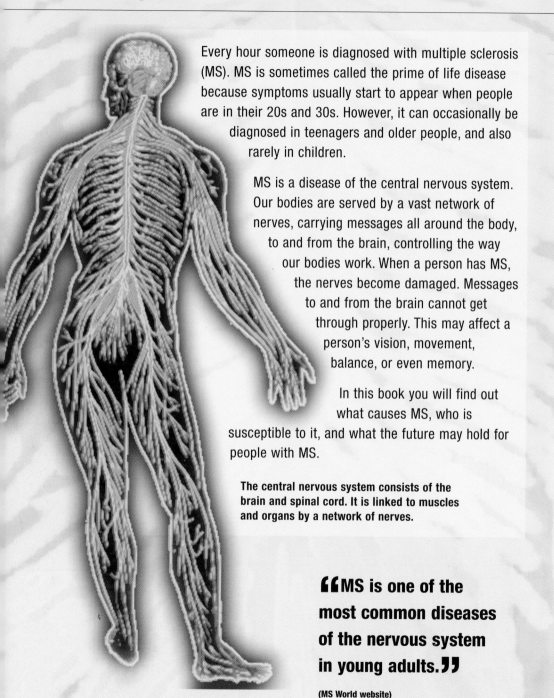

Every hour someone is diagnosed with multiple sclerosis (MS). MS is sometimes called the prime of life disease because symptoms usually start to appear when people are in their 20s and 30s. However, it can occasionally be diagnosed in teenagers and older people, and also rarely in children.

MS is a disease of the central nervous system. Our bodies are served by a vast network of nerves, carrying messages all around the body, to and from the brain, controlling the way our bodies work. When a person has MS, the nerves become damaged. Messages to and from the brain cannot get through properly. This may affect a person's vision, movement, balance, or even memory.

In this book you will find out what causes MS, who is susceptible to it, and what the future may hold for people with MS.

The central nervous system consists of the brain and spinal cord. It is linked to muscles and organs by a network of nerves.

"MS is one of the most common diseases of the nervous system in young adults."

(MS World website)

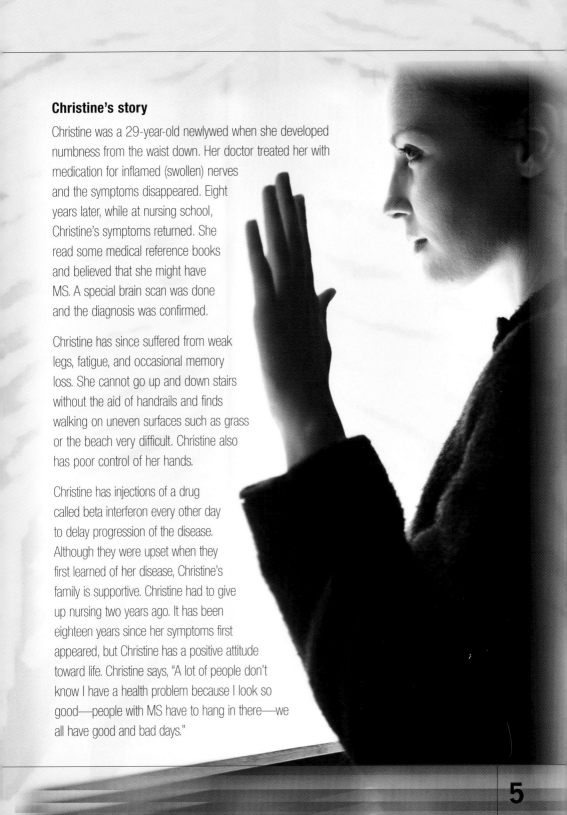

Christine's story

Christine was a 29-year-old newlywed when she developed numbness from the waist down. Her doctor treated her with medication for inflamed (swollen) nerves and the symptoms disappeared. Eight years later, while at nursing school, Christine's symptoms returned. She read some medical reference books and believed that she might have MS. A special brain scan was done and the diagnosis was confirmed.

Christine has since suffered from weak legs, fatigue, and occasional memory loss. She cannot go up and down stairs without the aid of handrails and finds walking on uneven surfaces such as grass or the beach very difficult. Christine also has poor control of her hands.

Christine has injections of a drug called beta interferon every other day to delay progression of the disease. Although they were upset when they first learned of her disease, Christine's family is supportive. Christine had to give up nursing two years ago. It has been eighteen years since her symptoms first appeared, but Christine has a positive attitude toward life. Christine says, "A lot of people don't know I have a health problem because I look so good—people with MS have to hang in there—we all have good and bad days."

What Is MS?

An estimated 400,000 people in the United States—and up to 2.5 million worldwide—have MS. About one in 1,000 people of European origin have the disease.

A disease of the central nervous system

MS is a disease that targets the central nervous system—the brain and the spinal cord. The brain is the control center for the whole body. Messages from the brain travel down the spinal cord to the muscles in the body and limbs. Messages also travel back to the brain up the spinal cord from the skin and joints. These messages travel along the nerves as electrical impulses. Some tell muscles to move and control how they work together. Other nerves from the skin and joints alert the brain to sensations such as vibration, temperature, pain, and the body's position.

A healthy spinal cord consists of nerves that conduct messages to and from the brain.

Nerves are protected by a fatty, insulating substance called myelin. In people with MS, some of the myelin is damaged. The electrical impulses are blocked in different parts of the brain, spinal cord, and nerves.

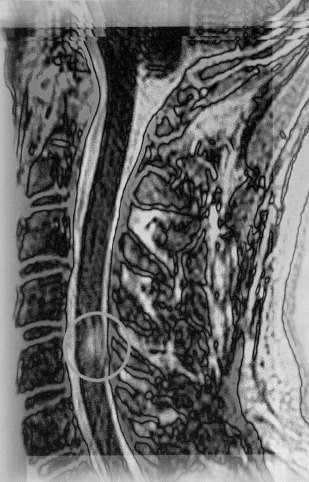

This spinal cord has been damaged by MS. A lesion (scar) is circled in pink, just to the right of the spine.

occur in MS are not predictable. They come and go and are not the same for everyone with the disease. In a mild case a person might simply have periods of intense fatigue; in severe cases they may be paralyzed.

Nerve cells under attack

The word *sclerosis* means "scarring." To someone looking at the brain or spinal-cord tissue of a person with MS, the disease looks like many scars. Some damage that occurs in MS is thought to be caused by an abnormal response to infections. The immune system (the body's natural defense system) produces white blood cells that destroy harmful bacteria or viruses. Many scientists believe that when some people with MS develop infections, the white blood cells function abnormally, attacking healthy tissue such as myelin and nerve cells. The destruction of healthy tissue by the immune system is called an autoimmune response.

When electrical impulses are blocked, nerves cannot carry their signals effectively. This is what causes the early symptoms of MS, such as weakness, numbness, loss of balance, or loss of vision. But, unlike many other diseases, the symptoms that

History of MS

People have probably suffered from MS throughout history. It was not until the 1860s, though, that the symptoms were linked to a specific disease. Before MS was recognized as a disorder of the central nervous system, people were sometimes referred to as having the "creeping paralysis," because symptoms mysteriously crept up on a person over a period of time.

Early cases

One of the earliest recorded cases of possible MS was a woman who became known as the Virgin Lidwina of Schiedam, Holland (1380–1433). She was the daughter of a laborer and one of nine children. Details of her illness came from her biographer, the Franciscan priest Johannes Brugman (1400–1473), who acquired information from relatives, her priest and confessor, and local clerics. Lidwina developed a series of MS-like symptoms following a fall while ice skating when she was sixteen. For the rest of her life she experienced unpleasant pains and difficulties with walking and using her arms. She developed blindness and had problems swallowing. She also had some strange hallucinations.

During her life she believed that her illness was sent by God and that she was a victim for the sins of others. After her death, a chapel was built on her grave. She was eventually made a saint for her suffering and patience, and is regarded as the patron saint of ice skaters.

Another early case of MS, of which there is now no doubt about the diagnosis, is that of Sir Augustus

Jean-Martin Charcot (fourth figure from the right) teaching at the University Hospital in Paris.

D'Este (1794–1848). He was the grandson of King George III of England and a cousin of Queen Victoria. It is believed that he was the first person ever to be diagnosed with MS after he had died. He suffered initially from blurred vision and then developed fatigue (excessive tiredness, often associated with MS), heat intolerance, spasms, and difficulty walking. He eventually used a wheelchair to get around. He died 26 years after his first symptoms appeared. His diary, which describes his experiences with the disorder, is now in the collection of the Royal College of Physicians in London.

In 1868 a French scientist, Jean-Martin Charcot, first recognized and defined MS. Sometimes referred to as the "Father of MS," Charcot was one of the founders of the science of neurology (the study of disorders of the nervous system). He demonstrated that there was a link between patients' symptoms and areas of inflammation and scarring in certain parts of the brain and spinal cord.

New discoveries

While Jean-Martin Charcot was the first to recognize MS as a disease, he never understood what caused it or how it might be treated. Many more discoveries were made during the 20th century. Each new discovery is like a piece of

Lord Edgar D. Adrian (right) won the Nobel Prize for Medicine in 1932.

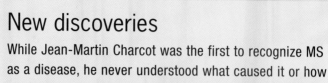

a jigsaw puzzle, and the picture of MS gradually becomes clearer as the pieces are put together.

In 1916 Dr. James Dawson of Edinburgh University in Scotland examined the brains of people who had died of MS, using a newly discovered way of viewing nerve cells under a microscope. A fatty substance surrounding nerves, myelin, had first been discovered in 1878 by the French anatomist Louis-Antoine Ranvier, but Dawson was now able to see this substance in detail. He noted that there was inflammation around the blood vessels and damage to the myelin around some nerves in the brains of the MS sufferers. This is a key feature of MS.

In 1925 British researcher Lord Edgar Douglas Adrian discovered that nerves carry electrical impulses (which we now know carry messages from the brain to different parts of the body and back again).

Working with others, he showed that these impulses were impaired when the surrounding myelin became damaged. Lord Adrian, together with Sir Charles Scott Sherrington, won the Nobel Prize for their discoveries about how nerve cells work.

Research on animals

In 1935 Dr. Thomas Rivers at the Rockefeller Institute in New York found a way of creating an MS-like disease in laboratory animals. This laboratory model of MS provided clues as to how MS worked. It led to the discovery that the body's natural defense system against disease (the immune system) could go wrong and attack its own tissue—the myelin.

Jigsaw puzzle

The discoveries in the early 20th century were the foundation of all modern research. More and more pieces of the MS puzzle have been put in place, but research into the disease has not yet been completed. When the last piece of the puzzle is in place, it will not be so much a breakthrough as the end result of hard and painstaking work carried out by scientists around the world for more than 100 years.

Types of MS

MS does not affect everyone in the same way. Symptoms may vary in severity, and not everyone will end up needing to use a wheelchair. There are four main types of MS: benign, relapsing/remitting (RRMS), secondary progressive (SPMS), and primary progressive.

Benign MS

Benign MS is the mildest form of MS. About ten to twenty percent of MS sufferers have benign MS. They may experience occasional attacks (called relapses) with periods of complete recovery (called remissions) in between. People with benign MS become only mildly disabled, and many have no disability at all. They have evidence of some MS damage on medical exams or brain scans but may experience very few symptoms. This is because the damage is either minimal or occurs in places in the brain or spinal cord that do not cause obvious disability.

Relapsing/remitting MS (RRMS)

More than half of people with MS begin with relapsing/remitting MS. They have relapses, roughly two or three times per year, with a partial or complete remission in between. But as time goes on, usually after several years, symptoms may worsen because of the gradual death of the nerve cells themselves, in addition to damage to the myelin sheaths surrounding them. At this stage the type of MS changes to SPMS.

Secondary progressive MS (SPMS)

Most people with RRMS eventually develop secondary progressive MS. After a few years, the frequency of relapses and remissions usually lessens, but the extent of disability increases due to the loss of the nerve cells. A person with MS is said to have SPMS when he or she no longer has relapses and remissions but experiences progressive disability instead. So this type of MS is called secondary because the disability has become progressive after several years of relapsing and remitting.

Primary progressive MS

About ten percent of people with MS become increasingly disabled over a period of several years without having any remissions. They gradually become more and more disabled without experiencing sudden worsening or periods of improvement in their symptoms. This type of MS is called primary progressive MS because progression is from the first symptom onward with no relapsing or remitting phase.

This woman has severe MS. Most people with the disease show fewer signs of disability.

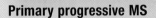

Diagnosis and Investigations

There is no definitive test for MS. A doctor must make a diagnosis based on several factors and rule out other possible conditions. The doctor builds up a picture of the disease until a diagnosis is possible.

Clues in a patient's medical history

If a patient has typical symptoms and signs of MS occurring in different parts of the brain and spinal cord at different times, a diagnosis of MS can sometimes be made from the patient's medical history. A person may have experienced a period of blurred vision at age twenty, for example, and two years later have a weak left leg together with a feeling of pins and needles in the right hand. This initial diagnosis will be followed up by a neurological examination. The doctor will test the patient's strength, vision, coordination, reflexes, and ability to feel different types of sensations. He or she looks for evidence of neurological damage, such as an extra jerky response to a tap under the knee or changes in the appearance of the optic nerve at the back of the eye.

Checking a person's knee-jerk reflexes can reveal damage in the spinal cord.

❝A disease does not exist until it has a name.❞
(Charles Rosenberg, professor of the history of science at Harvard University)

Investigations

The body's natural response to infection is to produce many white blood cells, which fight disease. In people with MS, the protective myelin covering nerve fibers also comes under attack from the white blood cells. One important laboratory test is the examination of the fluid that surrounds the brain and spinal cord (called cerebrospinal fluid). The fluid is extracted through a hollow needle that is inserted into the patient's spine in a procedure called a lumbar puncture. If the tests show an increase in white blood cells or a particular change in the chemical makeup of the cerebrospinal fluid, this can indicate that the patient has MS.

Another test for MS involves monitoring the electrical activity in the nerves connected with the patient's vision, hearing, or sensation of touch. A delay in electrical impulses traveling through a nerve, compared with what is normal in a healthy nerve, may indicate that the patient has MS.

Doctors also use a special brain scan—a magnetic resonance image (MRI) scan—to look for the hidden signs of MS. The MRI scanner uses a harmless magnetic field and radio waves to produce a detailed image of the brain and spinal cord. It can reveal damaged areas of myelin, called lesions.

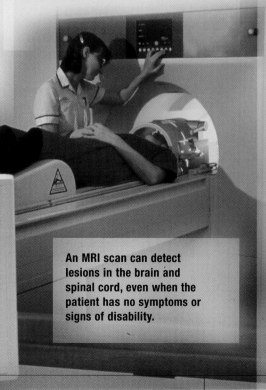

An MRI scan can detect lesions in the brain and spinal cord, even when the patient has no symptoms or signs of disability.

Symptoms of MS

Our spinal cords contain millions of nerves, all of which carry messages from the brain to different parts of the body and back again. Each nerve cell is protected by a myelin sheath. When a person has MS, the nerves' myelin becomes damaged, blocking the messages to and from the brain.

This may produce a wide range of symptoms depending on where in the body the nerve damage occurs.

Vision

Damage to one or both of the optic nerves (the nerves carrying messages from the eye to the brain and back again) may result in blurred vision. People with MS frequently suffer from eye problems but rarely lose their sight completely. Normal vision usually returns in four to twelve weeks, but some people with MS are left with

Blurred vision occurring suddenly in one eye is a common symptom of MS.

16

blind spots or more serious visual loss. Another common eye symptom is double vision. This can occur early on in MS, and people may remember having had this problem for many years before they developed other signs of the disease.

Sensation and pain

Another common symptom for people with MS is clumsiness of one arm. This is due to nerve damage in the spinal cord blocking the messages to and from the joints, fingers, and skin. A feeling of pins and needles, or numbness in the hands and feet, can be early symptoms of MS. Some people have burning or other types of pain in their legs, arms, or the trunk of their bodies. A few people experience a shooting, stabbing pain in the face, like a toothache. This form of neuralgia (nerve pain) affects the nerve carrying sensations from the face area. Other types of pain can occur in MS, often due to damaged nerves in a particular area of the body.

People with MS can find it difficult to pick things up because of impaired coordination.

Movement and balance

MS sufferers may also experience contraction and stiffness of muscles, affecting the arms, legs, and trunk of the body. This may result in painful muscle spasms. Most commonly this can affect the legs. In severe cases there is complete paralysis of a person's legs and they are unable to walk. Nerve damage in one part of the brain can cause balance problems and tremors (uncontrollable shaking). People who have difficulty with their balance still have some strength in their arms and legs, but they cannot control them properly. This makes it hard for them to handle objects or walk easily.

The MS bladder

Another common problem that MS sufferers experience is difficulty with bladder control. The bladder is controlled by several different nerves that connect to the muscles of the bladder. Nerve damage of the spinal cord can therefore lead to complicated urinary symptoms. The most common include frequent and urgent urination. Incontinence—when people cannot control when they urinate—can also be a problem. Our kidneys act as a natural filter system, removing impurities and waste products and passing them through the bladder and out of our bodies as urine. People with MS who have bladder control problems are more likely to get bladder or kidney infections as a result of stagnant urine in the bladder, so they must drink plenty of fluids.

Other symptoms

Some men and women with MS may experience difficulties in sexual relationships. The problems are caused by the nerves in the sexual organs, which do not function properly. People with MS, though, can still have children. Sometimes people with MS develop slurred speech and other communication problems. Some people may also find it difficult to swallow, and are at risk of chest infections if food goes down the wrong way and reaches the lungs. People who are paralyzed by MS and spend a lot of time in a wheelchair or in bed have a risk of developing bed sores. This is because the skin is deprived of blood and oxygen if a person stays in one

MS symptoms file

A person with MS may have three or four of the following symptoms, but not usually all at once:

- blurred or double vision
- loss of vision in one eye
- severe fatigue
- weakness of limbs, especially legs
- poor coordination and balance
- tremors
- dragging feet
- numbness and pins and needles
- burning sensations
- loss of bladder control
- difficulties with memory
- slurred speech.

For people with MS, exercise, heat, infections, and large meals can cause severe fatigue.

position for too long. But bed sores do not occur in people who have good nursing care.

Fatigue and memory

In addition to physical symptoms, MS can lead to memory difficulties, confusion, or emotional problems in some people. It also produces an overwhelming feeling of tiredness called MS fatigue.

Who Gets MS?

Why do some people get MS while others do not? MS is most likely to affect people living in the northernmost parts of the northern hemisphere and in the southernmost parts of the southern hemisphere. But if a person born in a low-risk area (such as South Africa) moves to a high-risk area (such as Canada) before they are fifteen, they have a greater risk of developing MS. However, if they leave South Africa after the age of fifteen, they are less likely to develop the disease.

This suggests that one factor influencing the development of MS may lie in the environment. This factor might be a local infection, something different about the local diet, or even different levels of sunshine.

Genetic factors?

Our genes contain the blueprint for everything about us, from height to eye color. Scientists believe that faulty genes have a role to play in passing on MS, although no specific genes have yet been identified.

Scientists do not yet understand why, but women are more likely to develop MS than men. In the United States the ratio is about two women to one man. While MS is not believed to be hereditary (directly passed on from a parent to a child), it does seem to run in families, which suggests that a susceptibility (tendency) to the disease can be inherited. MS is quite common in Scandinavia, but the Lapp people who live there develop it infrequently. They are of Asiatic origin and have a different genetic makeup than the fair-skinned peoples of the same region. We know that northern European populations are at greater risk for MS than African or Asian people. Similarly, no pure-blooded Aboriginal Australian, different in racial origin from Australians of European origin, has ever been diagnosed with MS.

When a person has MS, the whole family has to adjust and cope with the disease.

Did the Vikings spread MS?

One theory suggests that MS may have been carried and spread by the Vikings. The Vikings terrorized northern Europe in about 1000 C.E. Their descendants, including the Normans, later invaded and occupied many parts of the world. Wherever they went, they mixed with the local population and left many offspring to pass on their genes. MS is most common today in countries settled by people of northern European origin. While there is no conclusive genetic proof, the evidence is strong enough for some people to suggest that the Vikings spread MS.

How Does MS Develop?

When a person has MS, he or she develops lesions (areas of damage) in particular parts of the brain and spinal cord. These lesions are preceded by inflammation and an increase in white blood cells around certain nerve cells. The protective myelin sheath, which surrounds the nerve cell like a layer of insulation, is lost as a result of this process. When the myelin is damaged or lost, the electrical impulses (messages to and from the brain) traveling up or down the nerve are slowed down or stopped. Later, as the course of the disease develops, the nerve cells themselves may die. This is the reason why relapsing/remitting MS often develops into secondary progressive MS.

Nerve messages delayed or stopped

When there is nerve cell damage or loss, messages do not reach the brain from sensory areas in the skin, eyes, or joints. Other messages going from the brain to groups of muscles are also delayed or stopped. This interference

"One morning, about eight years ago, I awoke to find I could not see through my right eye. It was as though a film of cloud was covering it. I lay still for a while with my eyes closed, hoping that when I opened them all would be clear. Again, I opened my right eye, but with the same result."

(John Mythen, Canadian cartoonist and author of the cartoon book *Claude MSing Around*)

Tom's story

Tom is 49. He has primary progressive MS. Tom has experienced gradually increasing weakness in both legs over the last seven years. He also has difficulties controlling his bladder. He has never had a remission, and his condition has become progressively worse. Stiffness in his muscles is controlled by medication, but Tom now has to use a wheelchair to get around. He continues to work at a specially adapted office as a computer technician.

in the way nerves carry messages is responsible for the symptoms of MS. When such damage occurs in the brain or spinal cord, symptoms do not always develop. Sometimes, messages can find new pathways around the damage using other nerve cells. However, a few small lesions situated in important areas of the brain or spinal cord can cause more severe disability.

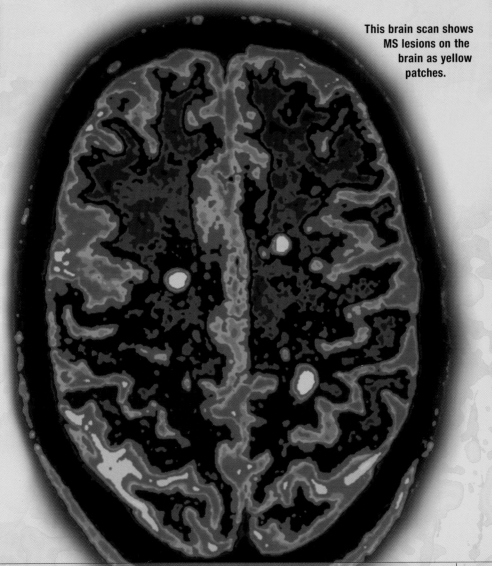

This brain scan shows MS lesions on the brain as yellow patches.

The mystery of what starts MS

The exact cause of MS remains a mystery. One theory suggests that MS might be the delayed effect of a virus acquired in childhood but causing damage years later. Another possibility is that the disease is started by an infection completely unlike a normal virus or bacterium. Such infections have been shown to cause other diseases of the central nervous system, such as Creutzfeld-Jacob disease (CJD).

Researchers have claimed that specific viruses have been identified in the microscopic examination of tissues from some people with MS. One virus under suspicion is human herpes virus 6 (HHV-6). The Epstein Barr Virus (EBV) may also be involved in causing MS. This virus is better known for causing glandular fever—a common throat infection in young people that leads to swollen and painful glands and a sore throat and causes general weakness and fatigue. At the moment, however, there is no scientific proof that any particular virus plays a part in MS. People with MS may have been infected by a combination of viruses.

Myelin sheaths (the fatty substance around nerves) enable electrical impulses to travel along the nerves quickly, taking messages to and from the brain.

The body's defenses go wrong

MS sufferers may have a genetic defect in their immune system, but scientists are not yet sure how this affects them. If a person's immune system is not functioning properly, it might allow a virus to remain in the body for longer than normal, or an attempt to rid the body of a virus might damage the body's own tissue. This is called an autoimmune response. It seems likely that an autoimmune response to an infection plays a part in the development of MS, as it does in the cases of other diseases such as diabetes.

In response to an infection, the immune system produces more white blood cells to fight against it. But if a person's immune system is not functioning properly, the white blood cells may also attack healthy tissue. In the case of MS it is the myelin surrounding nerve cells that is damaged. We know that MS relapses commonly occur after a viral infection such as a cold or the flu. This could mean that MS is made worse by all infections when they stimulate the body's immune system, further encouraging the production of destructive white blood cells.

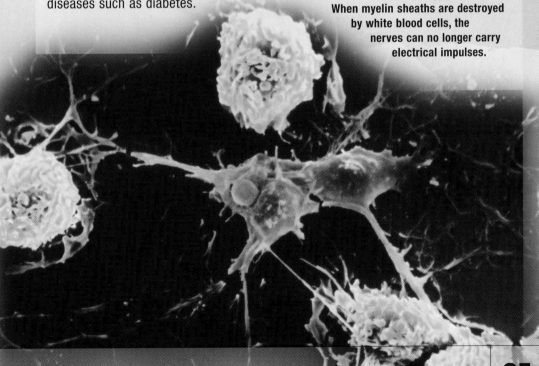

When myelin sheaths are destroyed by white blood cells, the nerves can no longer carry electrical impulses.

Managing MS

A person diagnosed with MS will see a wide range of professional people. Doctors and nurses help with the treatment and management of the disease. They work with other health and social workers when necessary. They also put MS sufferers in contact with local MS groups and the MS Society.

Doctors

The diagnosis of MS is made by a doctor who specializes in neurology (treatment of diseases of the central nervous system). He or she listens to the patient's symptoms, carries out a physical examination, and performs tests. It can take a long time to complete all the tests and this may be a period of anxiety and confusion for the patient and their family. The doctor keeps the patient informed of progress and confirms the diagnosis only when there is enough evidence.

Some people with MS can be shocked, skeptical, frightened, or angry when the condition is first diagnosed. They may feel that they have not been told quickly enough or they may even think that the neurologist has made a mistake. People can ask for another opinion about diagnosis or treatment if they want to. A good doctor will work in close partnership with his or her patient and respond to their fears and frustrations, taking the time to listen to the patient's questions about their condition. It is important that the person with MS is given information about the disease together with emotional support. The family

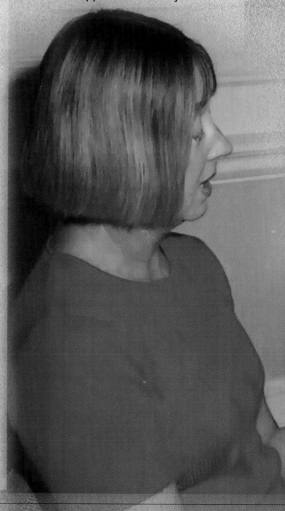

doctor will usually be the key person managing the treatment of MS after the diagnosis has been made. He or she will arrange whatever support and backup is needed.

Nurses and counselors

Sometimes a counselor will be able to help a person or family come to terms with MS and make life adjustments.

Counselors provide help and support. They are professionals in their own right, but much counseling is also done by the various health and social workers. Many people in families with MS find they have the resources to help each other without needing to involve counselors, but there should be regular contact with a trusted doctor to ensure the best possible long-term care is obtained.

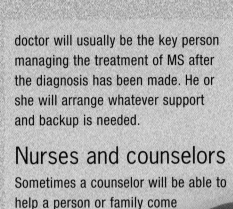

Continuing to work

When a person has MS, he or she usually hopes to continue working to make money for the family and continue to make a contribution to their community. Work is also important for a person's self-respect. MS has an impact on how well someone can work if he or she is disabled. It can also make getting to work, climbing stairs, and even using the toilet more difficult. People with MS are often affected by increasing tiredness, or fatigue, and this can lead to loss of concentration and affect a person's ability to do some types of work. People with MS can continue working when their difficulties are understood. A person's working space and method of working can be adapted to suit a particular disability.

Professor Barbara Jordan, a former U.S. congresswoman and businesswoman who had MS, lived a full and active life before her death in 1996.

Advice and therapy

An occupational therapist is a professional who can advise a person and his or her employer how to make helpful changes after the person's abilities and needs have been accessed. Simple changes can often make it possible for people with MS to continue to work.

A person can be given a work space closer to the bathroom, for example, or be provided with a desk where there is room for a wheelchair. Flexible working hours and a place for rest may also help.

Making it easier

People who have MS will often need help getting around. Cars can be specially adapted with hand controls instead of foot pedals, or people can use taxis or handicapped-accessible public transportation. Provisions can be made for wheelchairs, and elevators can be provided. Many countries have laws ensuring that

A wheelchair-adapted car can give a person with MS greater independence.

there is no discrimination against disabled people accessing and using the workplace, but employers and colleagues will want to help anyway. Many people with MS can continue working as long as there is goodwill and understanding and changes are made. Others may not be able to work as before. They can find fulfillment in other ways, such as by performing volunteer work, and may benefit from financial support from the government.

People with MS must care for themselves properly. This includes following a healthy diet, avoiding situations that make the condition worse, and sticking to advice given by health-care professionals.

Keeping fit and healthy

There is no specific diet that has been proven to affect the course of MS. However, there is some evidence that people with the disease should minimize their intake of animal fats and increase the amount of polyunsaturated fats and fish oils. It is most important to eat a well-balanced diet with plenty of fruit, vegetables, and fiber. Being overweight, smoking, and drinking too much alcohol can worsen MS symptoms.

Staying cool

Many people with MS function best in cool but not cold surroundings. They must avoid hot places and not use too many blankets or take hot baths, which all make symptoms worse. Traveling can create anxiety for people with MS. Organizing help in advance at airports and train stations is recommended.

If the travel destination is hot, the person with MS will need reliable air conditioning and access to proper health-care facilities.

Complementary therapies

Complementary therapies are not cures for MS, but they can improve a person's sense of well-being, give enjoyment, and relieve depression and feelings of isolation.

• Aromatherapy is a gentle form of massage using aromatic oils. It promotes relaxation and can help relieve stress.

• Reflexology involves massaging the feet in a special way. Some believe this improves a person's health and well-being.

• Music, art, or dance therapy helps increase a person's confidence, feelings of well-being, and self-respect.

• Massage involves squeezing and smoothing muscles in the client's body—particularly in the neck, back, arms, and legs. This helps to relax muscles, reduce spasms, and increase mobility.

• Yoga enables people to maximize the strength they have, to learn relaxation skills, and to improve general posture through stretching and meditation.

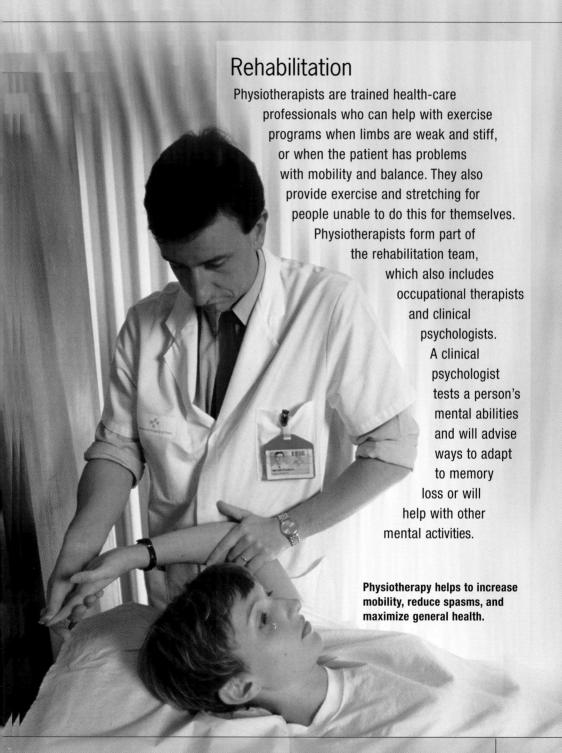

Rehabilitation

Physiotherapists are trained health-care professionals who can help with exercise programs when limbs are weak and stiff, or when the patient has problems with mobility and balance. They also provide exercise and stretching for people unable to do this for themselves. Physiotherapists form part of the rehabilitation team, which also includes occupational therapists and clinical psychologists. A clinical psychologist tests a person's mental abilities and will advise ways to adapt to memory loss or will help with other mental activities.

Physiotherapy helps to increase mobility, reduce spasms, and maximize general health.

Treating MS

People in the early stages of MS are often prescribed medication called corticosteroids. These can sometimes reduce the severity or length of a relapse. They work by reducing inflammation in nerve tissue and can be taken as pills or injected directly into a vein. They are given only for short periods because prolonged use causes side effects such as high blood pressure or weakened bones. Other medications are available to relax muscles and reduce muscle stiffening and spasms. Some can weaken the muscles too much, and a doctor must be careful to get the right dosage for the patient. Some medications can also help reduce MS fatigue.

Nerve stimulation

Functional electrical stimulation (FES) can also help some people with weak muscles. A small box sends electrical stimulation to paralyzed muscles to help the person regain useful movement. The FES box is connected to a pressure pad in a shoe that enables the impulse to be triggered when walking, improving mobility.

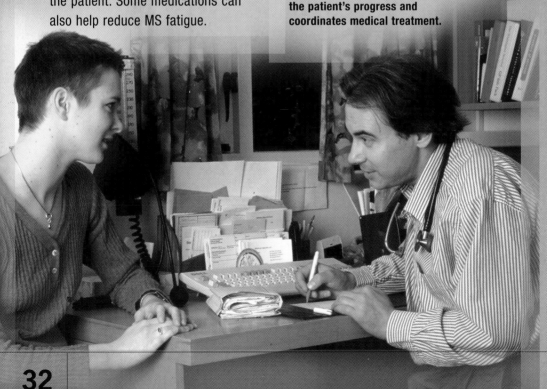

The family doctor monitors the patient's progress and coordinates medical treatment.

Regaining bladder control

Difficulties with bladder control in MS can be a major problem. People feel embarrassed about incontinence and worry about leaving their homes to work or socialize. This can make them feel very isolated, a disability in itself. But help is available. Some medications can relax the bladder muscles. Absorbent pads can be used if the problem continues. There are also various urine-collecting devices available that connect to bags worn under a person's clothes. But if medication alone does not work, there is an effective way of regaining continence. The person with MS can be trained to insert a sterile catheter—a thin, slippery plastic tube—into his or her bladder. This is called intermittent self-catheterization (ISC). The tube is inserted through the penis in men and through the urethral opening in women. This is done every four or five hours, completely emptying the bladder.

Good personal hygiene is essential to avoid the risk of infection.

"With proper symptom management, people rarely need to be treated for MS in a hospital."

(The Multiple Sclerosis Trust, 2002)

33

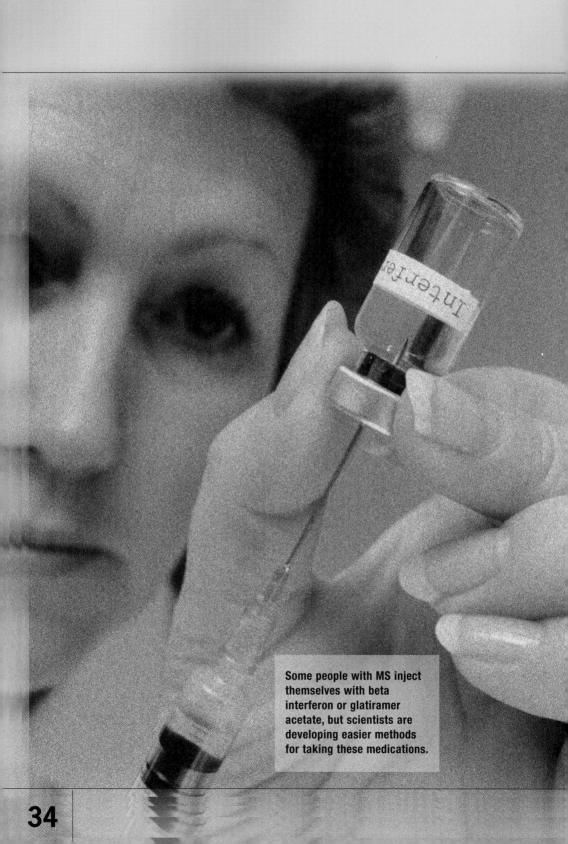

Some people with MS inject themselves with beta interferon or glatiramer acetate, but scientists are developing easier methods for taking these medications.

New medicines for MS

There is no cure for MS, but new medications are available that slow down the disease when relapses are frequent and especially disabling. Beta interferon is a genetically engineered copy of a protein that occurs naturally in the body. It is given by injection and works by regulating the immune system and by fighting viral infections. Research has shown that taking beta interferon can reduce the severity and frequency of relapses by 30 percent. This greatly increases the quality of a person's life. However, beta interferon does not reverse damage and has not been proven to prevent permanent disability.

An alternative to beta interferon is glatiramer acetate. This medication works by preventing myelin damage, and it must be injected once a day. Another disease-modifying medication is Novantrone. This drug suppresses the immune system. However, it can cause serious side effects and is only given in severe cases. It is administered directly into a vein every three months.

False treatments

Unfortunately, there are many claims by ignorant or unscrupulous people of other treatments and cures. People with MS and family members want to believe that these cures will work and will often spend a lot of money on treatments for which there is no scientific proof. They may become disappointed or angry when they do not work, or they may believe that they really do work and try to convince others. Examples of these misleading claims include removing all the mercury fillings from teeth or sitting in an oxygen chamber for hours at a time.

Many people with MS have remissions that occur naturally for no obvious reason. They may think they have discovered a cure if they are trying out a new, so-called treatment at the time of a natural remission.

Living with MS

People vary in the way they deal with MS. Some people become quite disabled but appear to adjust well and live a positive and rewarding life. Others with less disability may experience unhappiness and a feeling that life has become meaningless.

Coming to terms with MS

How a person copes often depends on his or her personality and how well they have adjusted to past problems. A perfectionist, for example, may find it more difficult to accept change than a person who has a happy-go-lucky approach to life.

The way a person deals with MS might also depend on how much help he or she gets from family and friends. Someone living alone with little family contact may cope well if he or she has understanding and supportive friends. But a person living at home may feel trapped and frustrated if family members try to protect the person too much and do everything for him or her.

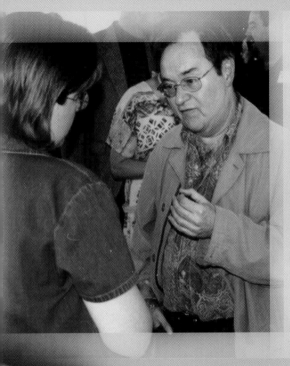

"I know, at first, when I was diagnosed with it I couldn't say 'multiple sclerosis.' Not because I have MS but just the thought of admitting to this disease, it sounded so powerful just saying the words that I just couldn't get myself to say it at first . . . I kept my MS a secret for fifteen years."

(Actor David Lander, pictured left, who played "Squiggy" on the TV show "Laverne & Shirley" and who has MS)

Many MS sufferers find the constant uncertainty about when the next relapse will strike very stressful. It takes time for people to come to terms with MS and adjust to a new image of themselves. Many are shocked when they first find out they have MS. They can find it hard to believe and accept, and they get angry with those around them. But more often they go through a period of sadness and loss until they come to accept MS as something they can live with. They need to keep a balance between giving in to MS and trying to pretend it is not there. But with understanding and support, a person who has MS will often be able to come to terms with it.

MS Fatigue

Everyone feels tired some of the time, but for people with MS the sensation of fatigue is more extreme. It is a special type of tiredness due to muscle weakness and the impaired functioning of the brain, spinal cord, and nerves. This is one of the symptoms that people with MS find most distressing and disabling.

The heat effect

MS fatigue can develop quickly when a person exercises or gets hot, such as when they travel to a hot country or if they get an infection. People vary in how much fatigue they have, and not everyone with MS is exhausted in the same way or by the same conditions. People affected by MS fatigue may feel very tired. They usually experience some worsening of symptoms and have difficulty concentrating. They may get into a bathtub full of hot water feeling fine—but after a few minutes they may begin to feel tired and weak. When they try to get out of the tub they may struggle and need help because of weakness in the legs and difficulty with balancing. In addition, they may find their vision is blurred and they have a pins and needles feeling in their hands. Although it does not take long for the fatigue to start, it can take a long time for it to go—they have to cool down first. People with MS are most likely to feel fatigued in the afternoon, when the body's natural temperature cycle is at its highest and also after big meals.

Larry

Larry is 60 years old. He has a mild form of MS known as benign MS. His main problem is MS fatigue. He always looks perfectly normal, and no one could ever guess that he has had MS for 25 years. His vision is occasionally blurred, especially after a hot bath or in a summer heat wave, but otherwise he feels healthy and enjoys going for long walks with his family and dogs.

This patient is being monitored as he exercises in cool water. This is part of a scientific research program to monitor the effect of heat on MS fatigue.

Misunderstanding fatigue

Because fatigue is invisible to other people, they may not be very sympathetic. Friends sometimes remark how good a person with MS looks, and suggest that the person is exaggerating his or her symptoms. People with MS are occasionally told that they are seeking attention or making it up. Words like these can undermine the trust in relationships with family, friends, and professionals.

Other Problems

Depression

Having MS can make people feel anxious and stressed, especially at the beginning when there is much uncertainty about what is going to happen to them. People with MS can go through periods of sadness and hopelessness. When these feelings are deep and last for more than two weeks, they may be symptoms of clinical depression. People with depression will often find it difficult to sleep or enjoy food. They lose their zest for life and may not have enough energy to cope with normal family life or work.

Memory loss and emotions

Some people with MS experience problems with their memory and concentration. These symptoms can be worrisome, both for those with the disease and for their families—especially if people do not understand that MS is the cause of the difficulties. These symptoms are produced when MS lesions affect the area at the front of the brain, which deals with thinking, emotions, and problem solving.

Some people with MS may lose control over their emotions. They may cry or laugh for no reason, and they may become frightened of overreacting in front of others. This is embarrassing and can lead to withdrawal from society. These symptoms, like the physical ones, come and go and are made worse by fatigue, infection, or stress.

Personality change

A few people with MS become disabled intellectually and are unable to carry out even simple tasks. This is rare and usually occurs in people who are also severely disabled by physical problems. A few people with MS have a lesser degree of intellectual impairment. People may not understand why they appear to be self-centered and inconsiderate of other people's needs.

These symptoms occur when someone with MS loses his or her ability to understand the feelings of others. Rarely, MS can produce serious psychiatric conditions such as bipolar disorder, a form of depression in which a person alternates between being deeply depressed and very excited.

MS and the Family

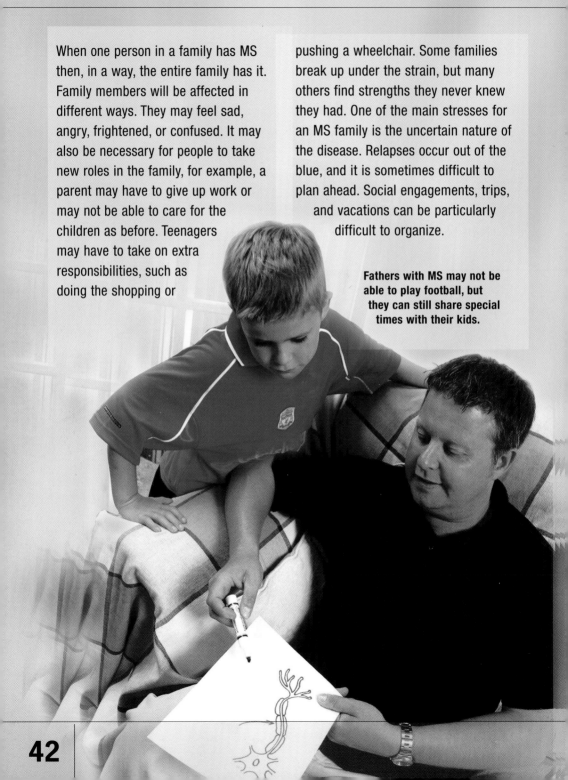

When one person in a family has MS then, in a way, the entire family has it. Family members will be affected in different ways. They may feel sad, angry, frightened, or confused. It may also be necessary for people to take new roles in the family, for example, a parent may have to give up work or may not be able to care for the children as before. Teenagers may have to take on extra responsibilities, such as doing the shopping or pushing a wheelchair. Some families break up under the strain, but many others find strengths they never knew they had. One of the main stresses for an MS family is the uncertain nature of the disease. Relapses occur out of the blue, and it is sometimes difficult to plan ahead. Social engagements, trips, and vacations can be particularly difficult to organize.

Fathers with MS may not be able to play football, but they can still share special times with their kids.

The children of parents with MS can be particularly affected. They may feel ignored and want more attention at home or at school. Some feel confused about what has happened to their parent. They may worry that they will catch MS themselves, or that it is somehow their fault that their parent has MS. Children sometimes feel unreasonably guilty if their mother's illness developed after their birth. Teenagers may find themselves taking on the job of caring for a parent. This can be tiring and lonely work, and it can be difficult for them to go out or have friends over.

Pregnancy

When a woman with MS becomes pregnant, she may feel fine during pregnancy, but she is more likely to have a relapse after the birth. However, having a baby does not make a woman's MS worse in the long term, although it may be difficult for her to find the energy and strength to care for her children. Most MS families find their own ways of getting by, and children of MS families often mature into especially understanding and practical people.

"They came home and told my sister and me. Di and I went into the kitchen, cried, and swore that we were going to behave like angels from then on—a resolution I think we broke within 48 hours."

(J. K. Rowling, author of the Harry Potter books, describing her feelings after learning her mother had MS. She is pictured here in 2001 at an event hosted by the MS Society.)

MS and Society

Society sometimes treats people with disabilities as second-class citizens. In the past, people with disabilities were kept out of sight or even feared. Even today, they are sometimes avoided, talked down to, ignored, or expected to accept second best. Such negative attitudes can make it more difficult for people with MS to adjust to a new role in life or to ask for help. But when a community welcomes people with disabilities and understands their problems, people with MS can feel like they belong. Of course, people with MS are all different individuals with their own strengths and weaknesses, but society can help them to take a full part in everyday life, which in turn can help them to accept their own destiny.

The price of independence

MS costs everyone money because of the extra need for medical and social care and government funds. But if people are helped to be independent and to continue working, they can make their own contribution to the community. They feel better, they contribute more, and it costs the community less. Help with transportation and easy access to buildings can make a big difference. People with more serious disabilities

Some MS groups sponsor walks or other activities to have fun and raise money for research. This walk took place in 1999 in Community Park, Jacksonville, Illinois.

may need special adaptations to their home, such as a ramp for getting a wheelchair in and out, and this can help them to continue living on their own. Some people even have specially trained assistance dogs to help with day-to-day tasks.

Self help

There are many groups that help people with MS to help themselves and each other. In many countries such as the United States, the United Kingdom, and Canada, MS charities give information, support, social contacts, and wide-ranging advice. These groups also provide opportunities for self-help and they campaign for special causes, funding for new treatments, and fairer laws for people with disabilities. The Internet provides even more ways for a person to find information, look up medical research, and make contact with others. Even people who are mostly housebound can make friends and contacts in MS chat rooms, and feel that they are playing a valuable part in the world community of people who have MS.

Will a Cure Be Found?

Research into MS is carried out worldwide and often funded by governments, pharmaceutical companies, or MS charities. The National MS Society of the United States has supported research since 1946 and now spends about $320 million a year on carefully selected research programs. There are four main areas of study—immunology, genetics, virology, and the biology of myelin.

Immunology

Immunology research is now concentrated on determining exactly which specific immune responses lead to MS. In the future this is likely to lead to safer, more effective medications with fewer side effects.

Genes

No specific gene has been found to cause MS. MS is likely to be the result of many genes affecting different aspects of the disease process. Researchers are now comparing the genetic makeup of individuals, twins, and ethnically diverse populations. In this way it is hoped to find the difference in the genetic makeup of various people who are more or less likely to develop the disease. One day this might mean that gene abnormalities can be prevented or corrected by gene therapy—this means actually changing the genes a person has or modifying how they work. Research, though, is still in its very early stages.

Viruses and the immune system

Experts in virology and bacteriology now believe that the immune system in people with MS may deal abnormally with many different types of infection. Learning how the immune systems of individual people deal with infections may lead to further understanding of what goes wrong and how to prevent an inappropriate autoimmune response so that white blood cells do not attack healthy myelin.

Nerves and myelin

Myelin research is being carried out to determine what factors play a part in nerve damage, how to stop this process, and how to repair the myelin. Scientists are even looking at ways to make nerve cells grow again.

The search for a cure must continue. Sometimes answers come unexpectedly from seemingly unrelated fields within basic biomedical research; more often the route is slow and arduous.

(Sylvia Lawry, founder of the National Multiple Sclerosis Society and the Multiple Sclerosis International Federation)

Immunologists are working on research into MS.

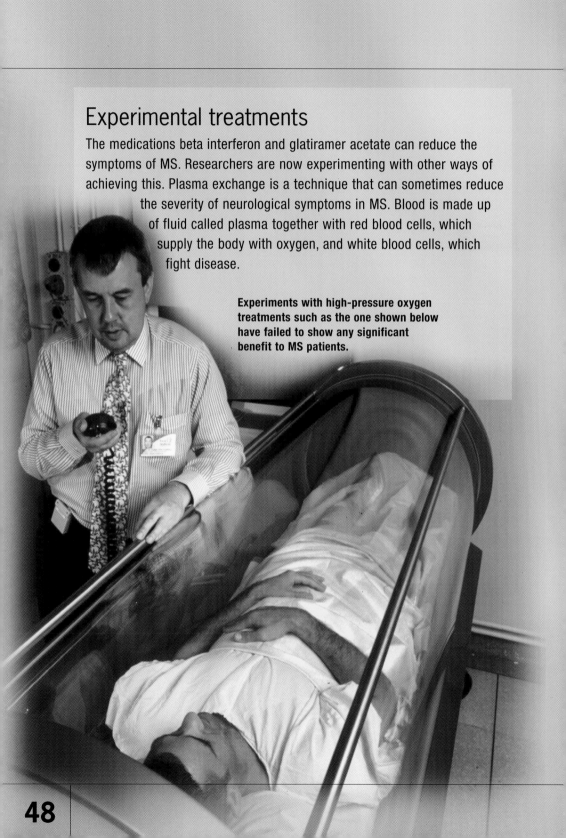

Experimental treatments

The medications beta interferon and glatiramer acetate can reduce the symptoms of MS. Researchers are now experimenting with other ways of achieving this. Plasma exchange is a technique that can sometimes reduce the severity of neurological symptoms in MS. Blood is made up of fluid called plasma together with red blood cells, which supply the body with oxygen, and white blood cells, which fight disease.

Experiments with high-pressure oxygen treatments such as the one shown below have failed to show any significant benefit to MS patients.

Plasma from a person with MS may contain poisonous substances that make MS worse. The plasma exchange procedure separates the patient's blood cells from the plasma. The cells are then mixed with plasma obtained from donors (healthy people without a disease), and the new mixture is put back into the bloodstream. Antiviral medications are also being tried and may have a role to play in reducing the symptoms of fatigue.

People often feel better if they are given any type of treatment, even one that has been shown to have no effect on a disease. Research into any new treatment takes this into consideration. To test the reliability of a new drug, it must be compared with a placebo—a substance that looks exactly the same, but is known to be ineffective. During the drug trials, the placebo and the medicine to be tested are labeled in code. Neither the people receiving the substances nor the doctors giving them know which is the real drug. At the end of a trial, which may take several years, the researchers unlock the codes and can see if there is a genuine effect. All new treatments for MS are tested in this way to make sure that they are both safe and effective.

Marijuana—the debate

One controversial study is looking into the effectiveness of marijuana (pictured below) in the treatment of MS. Marijuana has been used medicinally for over 2,000 years but is now illegal in most countries. However, some people with MS claim that marijuana helps reduce their symptoms, especially muscle spasms. In 1998 the House of Lords, in the United Kingdom, looked at the issue of the medicinal use of marijuana and recommended further studies. Since that time, research trials have been set up to find out if these claims are true.

The future is bright

A diagnosis of MS may mean disability, but for most people it is not a death sentence and many will never need a wheelchair. In the last twenty years, scientists have learned a great deal about who gets MS, how the disease affects people, and what the possible causes might be. MS is not yet curable, but there are treatments available that can lessen or eliminate some of the symptoms.

There are also many ways to improve general health and mobility to make it possible for people with MS to live almost normal lives. Sadly, some people are more severely affected by MS, but society is gradually finding better ways to help physically, emotionally, and financially.

Research into the disease continues, often supported by voluntary MS organizations. While we do not yet have all the answers, the pieces of the puzzle are coming together. We can see how genetic and environmental factors might combine to produce MS.

Genes perhaps cause an abnormal response to infection, and instead of just fighting the infection they also cause damage to the central nervous system. It is a bit like an army fighting an enemy but getting the wrong instructions and attacking its own side.

This ten-year-old boy (right) has MS, but it is rare for the disease to affect children.

In the future, there is good reason to believe that we will find ways of treating MS more effectively or even preventing the disease before it can do any damage. Information about MS is now readily available to everyone. It is important that people with MS fully understand the disease. Knowing the facts about MS empowers people to come to terms with the illness and seek out effective and scientifically proven ways to fight this destructive and disabling condition.

"Even with my physical limitations, I know that there is so much I can do."

(Karen Model, who has MS, attending the Heuga Center, an organization in Edwards, Colorado, that helps people with MS develop exercise programs)

Information and Advice

Most countries have an MS Society or similar voluntary organizations, and there is also an international federation that supports and helps to develop these charities. MS Societies usually have local groups that provide direct help for people in the community. Many offer online discussion groups for people with MS and their relatives, including children and teenagers. There are also some good booklets and newsletters available for young people. It is worth checking with the charities directly to obtain the most up-to-date information on research, publications, and various support groups.

Contacts

National Multiple Sclerosis Society
733 Third Avenue
New York, NY 10017
Phone: 800-344-4867
Website: www.nationalmssociety.org
The mission of the National Multiple Sclerosis Society is to end the devastating effects of MS.

Multiple Sclerosis Foundation
6350 North Andrews Avenue
Fort Lauderdale, FL 33309-2130
Phone: 1-888-MSFOCUS
Website: Website: www.msfacts.org
The Multiple Sclerosis Foundation's mission is to ensure the best quality of life for those coping with MS by providing comprehensive support and educational programs.

Multiple Sclerosis International Federation
3rd Floor, Skyline House
200 Union Street
London SE1 0LX
Phone: +44 (0) 20 7620 1911
Website: www.msif.org
The Multiple Sclerosis International Federation was established in 1967 as an international body linking the activities of National MS Societies around the world.

Websites

All About Multiple Sclerosis
www.mult-sclerosis.org
All About Multiple Sclerosis aims to provide accurate and comprehensive medical information about multiple sclerosis written in plain English by people living with the disease and its symptoms.

Keep S'Myelin
www.nationalmssociety.org
keepsmyelin/index.html
This is a website for children of people who have MS.

MS World
www.msworld.org
The MS World worldwide Internet family includes thousands of people from around the world diagnosed with MS.

More Books to Read

Abramovitz, Melissa. *Multiple Sclerosis.* Farmington Hills, Mich.: Gale Group, 2002.

Aaseng, Nathan. *Multiple Sclerosis.* Danbury, Conn.: Scholastic Library, 2000.

Burnett, Betty, and Rob Gevertz. *Coping with Multiple Sclerosis.* New York: Rosen Publishing, 2001.

Gold, Susan Dudley. *Multiple Sclerosis.* Berkeley Heights, N.J.: Enslow Publishers, 2001.

Goldstein, Margaret J. *Everything You Need to Know about Multiple Sclerosis.* New York: Rosen Publishing, 2001.

Smith, Jennifer Crown. *Dad's Falling Apart: Keeping It Together When a Family Member Has Multiple Sclerosis.* Albuquerque, N.Mex.: Health Press, 2003.

Susman, Edward. *Multiple Sclerosis.* Berkeley Heights, N.J.: Enslow Publishers, 1999.

Glossary

autoimmune response
body's response in which the immune system attacks the body's own tissues

bed sore
damage to skin that occurs when a person lies or sits in one position for too long

benign
not harmful

beta interferon
drug used to lessen the effects of MS

bipolar disorder
mental illness in which severe depression alternates with periods of extreme excitement

catheter
tube inserted into the bladder for removal of urine

central nervous system
brain and spinal cord

cerebrospinal fluid (CSF)
fluid surrounding the brain and spinal cord

clinical depression
psychiatric illness in which a person becomes severely depressed and loses hope

clinical psychologist
professional trained to help a person with mental and behavioral difficulties

corticosteroid
medication that controls inflammation

Creutzfeld-Jacob Disease (CJD)
infectious disease of the brain, known as mad cow disease when it affects cattle

Epstein-Barr Virus (EBV)
common virus that may cause a sore throat and fatigue for several weeks (glandular fever)

functional electrical stimulation (FES)
process that uses special equipment to stimulate paralyzed muscles

gene
part of chromosomes that carries instructions for how the body develops and carries out life processes

glatiramer acetate
disease-modifying medication used to lessen the effects of MS

hallucination
false vision

hereditary
directly passed on from a parent to a child

human herpes virus 6 (HHV-6)
common virus that causes a rash called roseola in children

immune system
body's own self-defense system, which fights infection and provides resistance to disease

immunology
study of the immune system

incontinence
loss of control of the bladder

inflammation
condition in which a part of the body becomes red, sore, and swollen because of infection or injury

intermittent self-catheterization (ISC)
emptying the bladder by inserting a sterile tube when normal bladder control is unreliable

lesion
area of damage, such as a scar

lumbar puncture (spinal tap)
extracting a sample of the fluid surrounding the spinal cord

magnetic resonance image (MRI) scan
special type of scan using magnetic fields to produce an image

myelin
fatty substance protecting and surrounding the nerve fibers

neuralgia
intense nerve pain that comes and goes

neurological
dealing with disorders of the nervous system

neurology
study of nervous system disorders

Novantrone
medication used to lessen the immune response and so modify the MS disease

occupational therapist
expert in helping disabled people with problems in the workplace and everyday living

optic nerve
nerve connecting the eye to the brain

pharmaceutical
dealing with the production of medications

physiotherapist
expert who helps people with physical disabilities to restore or improve movement

placebo
substance with no medical action

plasma
liquid part of blood

polyunsaturated fat
food oil that helps nerves grow and work properly

primary progressive MS
gradually worsening MS without remissions

psychiatric
dealing with mental illness

rehabilitation
act of helping people (or helping oneself) to get back to normal life

relapse
sudden worsening of symptoms

relapsing/remitting MS (RRMS)
type of MS in which symptoms occur from time to time, then improve for a while before returning

remission
recovery from MS symptoms after a relapse or attack

sclerosis
area of scarring or hardening of tissue

secondary progressive MS (SPMS)
type of MS marked by gradual worsening after a period of relapses and remissions

spasm
involuntary muscle contraction

susceptibility
tendency

tremor
uncontrolled shaking

urinary
dealing with the bladder, the kidneys, and the passing of urine

virology
study of viruses

white blood cell
cell that fights infection

Index